rockschool®

A. Poole
9/7/16.

Acoustic Guitar
Grade 2

Performance pieces, technical exercises, supporting tests and in-depth guidance for Rockschool examinations

All accompanying and supporting audio can be downloaded from: *www.rslawards.com/downloads*

Input the following code when prompted: **WUQUXXWNSD**

For more information, turn to page 5

www.rslawards.com

Acknowledgements

Published by Rockschool Ltd. © 2016
Catalogue Number RSK200022
ISBN: 978-1-910975-29-9
Initial release | Errata details can be found at *www.rslawards.com*

SYLLABUS
Syllabus written and devised by Nik Preston and Andy G Jones
Syllabus consultants: Andy G Jones, Carl Orr and James Betteridge
Arrangements by Andy G Jones, Carl Orr and James Betteridge
Supporting Tests written by Nik Preston and Andy G Jones
Syllabus advisors: Simon Troup and Jamie Humphries

PUBLISHING
Fact Files written by Diego Kovadloff
Music engraving and book layout by Simon Troup and Jennie Troup of Digital Music Art
Proof reading and copy editing by Diego Kovadloff, Carl Orr and Mary Keene
Cover design by Philip Millard
Cover photograph © EDV/Splash News/Corbis

AUDIO
Produced by Nik Preston, Andy G Jones, Carl Orr and James Betteridge
Engineered by Andy G Jones, Carl Orr, James Betteridge, Jonas Persson and Music Sales
Mixed by Andy G Jones, Carl Orr, James Betteridge
Mastered by Ash Preston and Paul Richardson
Supporting Tests recorded by Andy G Jones
Executive producers: John Simpson and Norton York

MUSICIANS
Andy G Jones, Carl Orr, James Betteridge, Nik Preston, Ian Thomas, Mike Finnigan, Noel McCalla,
Patti Revell and Hannah Vasanth

SPONSORSHIP
Andy G Jones endorses Thomastik Infeld strings, Providence cables and pedal switching systems, Free The Tone effects,
JJ Guitars, Ergoplay guitar supports and Wampler Pedals. All nylon strings parts recorded direct with the Yamaha NTX2000.
Carl Orr endorses MI Audio Revelation amps & effects, and Picato strings.
James Betteridge plays Martin guitars and D'addario strings.

DISTRIBUTION
Exclusive Distributors: Music Sales Ltd

CONTACTING ROCKSCHOOL
www.rslawards.com
Telephone: +44 (0)345 460 4747
Email: *info@rslawards.com*

Table of Contents

Introductions & Information

Rockschool Grade Pieces

Technical Exercises

Supporting Tests

Additional Information

Welcome to Rockschool Acoustic Guitar Grade 2

Welcome to **Rockschool's 2016 Acoustic Guitar syllabus**. This syllabus has been designed to equip all aspiring guitarists with a range of stylistically appropriate, industry relevant skills and a thoroughly engaging learning experience.

Utilising an array of well known repertoire and a truly crucial range of supporting tests, the continued progression of any student is assured from Debut through to Grade 8.

The syllabus has been authored to ensure that each student can develop as accompanists, soloists, sight readers and improvisers, whilst enabling both teacher and student to choose the areas that they wish to specialise in.

Rockschool's long standing commitment to raising academic standards, assessing industry-relevant skills and ensuring student engagement is world renowned. The 2016 Acoustic Guitar syllabus has been conceived in order to build upon this success and continue the evolution of the contemporary music world's first awarding body.

When combined with **Rockschool's 2015 Popular Music Theory syllabus**, this syllabus is guaranteed to furnish every candidate with both the practical skills and theoretical understanding necessary to perform at the highest level, across a whole range of contemporary repertoire.

Nik Preston – Head of Product Development and Publishing

Acoustic Guitar Exams

At each grade you have the option of taking one of two different types of examination:

- **Grade Exam**

  (Debut to Grade 5)

  A Grade Exam is a mixture of music performances, technical work and tests. You are required to prepare three pieces (two of which may be Free Choice Pieces) and the contents of the Technical Exercise section. This accounts for 75% of the exam marks. The other 25% consists of: either a Sight Reading or an Improvisation & Interpretation test (10%), two Ear Tests (10%), and finally you will be asked five General Musicianship Questions (5%). The pass mark is 60%.

  (Grades 6–8)

  A Grade Exam is a mixture of music performances, technical work and tests. You are required to prepare three pieces (two of which may be Free Choice Pieces) and the contents of the Technical Exercise section. This accounts for 75% of the exam marks. The other 25% consists of: a Quick Study Piece (10%), two Ear Tests (10%), and finally you will be asked five General Musicianship Questions (5%). The pass mark is 60%.

- **Performance Certificate**

  A Performance Certificate is equivalent to a Grade Exam, but in a Performance Certificate you are required to perform five pieces. A maximum of three of these can be Free Choice Pieces. Each song is marked out of 20 and the pass mark is 60%.

Book Contents

The book is divided into a number of sections:

- **Exam Pieces**

  Each exam piece is preceded by a Fact File detailing information about the original recording, the composer and the artist/s who performed it. There is also a Technical Guidance section at the end of each piece which provides insight from the arrangers as to the harmonic, melodic, rhythmic and technical nuance of each piece.

  Every exam piece is notated for acoustic guitar, but certain pieces feature two 'assessed' parts, meaning the candidate has the choice of which part they wish to perform in the exam. Certain pieces contain 'non-assessed' guitar parts, which are intended for duet/ensemble practice and performance. Likewise, certain pieces include notated vocal melodies in addition to the assessed guitar part. These have been included as reference material and to provide opportunity for duet and ensemble practice and performance. In your exam you must perform your pieces to the backing tracks provided.

- **Technical Exercises**

  There are either three or four types of technical exercise, depending on the grade:

  Group A – scales

  Group B – arpeggios/broken chords

  Group C – chord voicings

  Group D – a choice of stylistic studies. Please note, Group D only exists at Grades 6–8.

- **Supporting Tests**

  You are required to undertake three kinds of unprepared, supporting test:

  1. Sight Reading or an Improvisation & Interpretation test at Debut to Grade 5.
     Please note, these are replaced by mandatory Quick Study Pieces (QSPs) at Grades 6–8.

  2. Ear Tests: Debut to Grade 3 feature Melodic Recall and Chord Recognition.
     Grades 4–8 feature Melodic Recall and Harmonic Recall.

  3. General Musicianship Questions (GMQs), which you will be asked by the examiner at the end of each exam.
     Each book features examples of the types of unprepared tests likely to appear in the exam.
     The examiner will give you a different version in the exam.

- **General Information**

  You will find information on exam procedures, including online examination entry, marking schemes, information on Free Choice Pieces and improvisation requirements for each grade.

Audio

In addition to the Grade book, we have also provided audio in the form of backing tracks (minus assessed guitar part) and examples (including assessed guitar part) for both the pieces and the supporting tests where applicable. This can be downloaded from RSL directly at *www.rslawards.com/downloads*

You will need to input this code when prompted: **WUQUXXWNSD**

The audio files are supplied in MP3 format. Once downloaded you will be able to play them on any compatible device.

You can find further details about Rockschool's Acoustic Guitar syllabus by downloading the syllabus guide from our website: *www.rslawards.com*

All candidates should download and read the accompanying syllabus guide when using this grade book.

Acoustic Guitar Notation Explained

THE MUSICAL STAVE shows pitches and rhythms and is divided by lines into bars. Pitches are named after the first seven letters of the alphabet.

TABLATURE graphically represents the guitar fingerboard. Each horizontal line represents a string, and each number represents a fret.

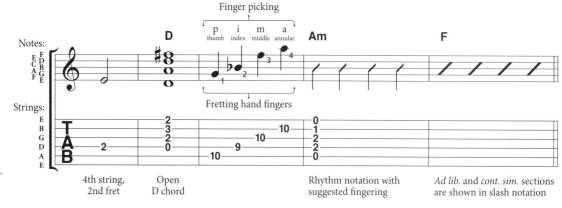

4th string, 2nd fret   Open D chord   Rhythm notation with suggested fingering   *Ad lib.* and *cont. sim.* sections are shown in slash notation

Definitions For Special Guitar Notation

HAMMER ON: Pick the lower note, then sound the higher note by fretting it without picking.

PULL OFF: Pick the higher note then sound the lower note by lifting the finger without picking.

SLIDE: Pick the first note, then slide to the next with the same finger.

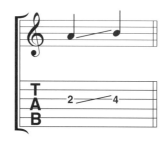

STRING BENDS: Pick the first note then bend (or release the bend) to the pitch indicated in brackets.

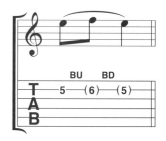

GLISSANDO: A small slide off of a note toward the end of its rhythmic duration. Do not slide 'into' the following note – subsequent notes should be repicked.

VIBRATO: Vibrate the note by bending and releasing the string smoothly and continuously.

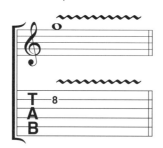

NATURAL HARMONICS: Lightly touch the string above the indicated fret then pick to sound a harmonic.

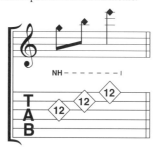

ARTIFICIAL HARMONICS: Fret the note indicated in the TAB, then (with picking hand) lightly touch the string above fret indicated between staves, and pick to sound the harmonic.

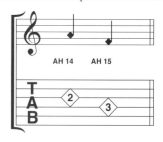

PRE-BENDS: Before picking the note, bend the string from the fret indicated between the staves, to the equivalent pitch indicated in brackets in the TAB

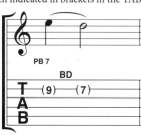

PICK HAND TAP: Strike the indicated note with a finger from the picking hand. Usually followed by a pull off.

FRET HAND TAP: As pick hand tap, but use fretting hand. Usually followed by a pull off or hammer on.

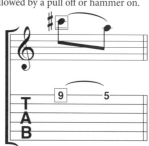

QUARTER TONE BEND: Pick the note indicated and bend the string up by a quarter tone.

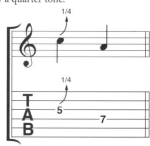

TRILL: Rapidly alternate between the two bracketed notes by hammering on and pulling off.

D.%. al Coda

- Go back to the sign (%), then play until the bar marked *To Coda* ✛ then skip to the section marked ✛ *Coda*.

D.C. al Fine

- Go back to the beginning of the song and play until the bar marked *Fine* (end).

- Repeat bars between signs.

- When a repeated section has different endings, play the first ending only the first time and the second ending only the second time.

Jimi Hendrix | All Along The Watchtower

SONG TITLE: ALL ALONG THE
WATCHTOWER

ALBUM: JOHN WESLEY HARDING

LABEL: COLUMBIA

GENRE: FOLK ROCK

WRITTEN BY: BOB DYLAN

GUITAR: BOB DYLAN

PRODUCER: BOB JOHNSON

UK CHART PEAK: 5 (HENDRIX'S VERSION)

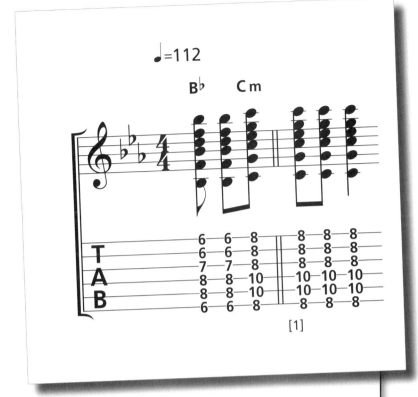

[1]

'All Along The Watchtower' was written by Bob Dylan during a period of convalescence in 1966. He spent a year and a half recuperating at home in Woodstock, after a motorcycle accident. The song stands in stark contrast to Dylan's previous work. It has a much darker and sparser feel. It was recorded in Nashville in 1967. The final version is made of two out of five takes. The song is highly regarded due to its mysterious lyrics, arguably related to biblical passages, and due to its unusual narrative structure. To some this reflects a complexity and mystique attributed to much of Dylan's work, to others it represents the randomness and erratic nature of much of the late 60's work. The song became a classic after Jimi Hendrix's rendition, released shortly after Dylan's. Hendrix's approach caught Dylan's attention and he decided to treat the song in Hendrix's fashion from then on.

Jimi Hendrix featured 'All Along The Watchtower' in his 1968 release *Electric Ladyland*. The version featured on the album was started in London in January of 1968 and finished at New York's Electric Ladyland studios, in August of the same year, after much overdubbing. Hendrix's recorded guitar solo has become legendary.

Jimi Hendrix is regarded as a pivotal figure in the world of rock for his virtuoso guitar playing and attitude. He revolutionised electric guitar playing and set the blueprint for many rock stars.

'All Along The Watchtower' has been covered by many artists since. These include U2, Dave Matthews and Neil Young.

"What struck me about the tunes that I had the opportunity to contribute to was the association with Robert Johnson and Jimi Hendrix, two of the most influential artists in the history of popular music. Both struck down at a young age, both still highly revered. Additionally, the Hendrix-inspired 'All Along The Watchtower' was written by perhaps the most influential songwriter in popular American music, Bob Dylan. I first heard Robert Johnson in 1965 when I was 20 years old. I'd grown up on R&B music, but had never heard Johnson, or any of the country blues which was the forerunner of so much later popular music.

Also, it was fun to perform 'Kind Hearted Woman' with Andy Jones. Having had the rare privilege of recording with Jimi Hendrix on his album 'Electric Ladyland', contributing to 'Watchtower' didn't seem as daunting a task! I'm grateful to be included in this project."

Mike Finnigan – Jimi Hendrix, Bonnie Raitt, Tower of Power, Rod Stewart, Ringo Starr, Cher.

All Along The Watchtower

Jimi Hendrix

Arranged by Andy G Jones

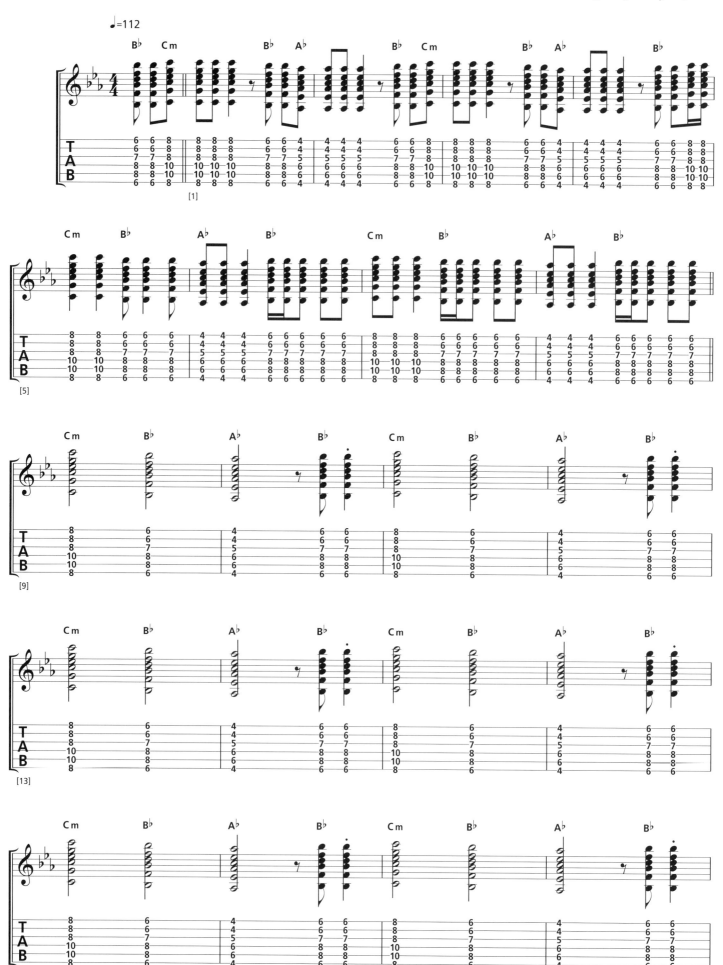

All Along The Watchtower | Technical Guidance

'All Along The Watchtower' by Jimi Hendrix is a workshop in blues/rock guitar. In this arrangement, rhythm is the main focus. The intro is similar to the one on Hendrix's original version. This section has confused many guitar players over the years. Beat one only becomes obvious when the drums set up the groove. The guitar comes in on the upbeat of beat 3 of the bar.

This tune is generally written in C♯ minor as Hendrix tuned his guitar down a semitone. The rest of the band would have played in concert C minor. This version is written at concert pitch.

In the intro, note how the rhythms are varied with semiquavers at the end of bar 5 and also syncopated in bar 6. This whole piece is based on three chords presented in a two bar loop. Jimi Hendrix is so inventive that the listener forgets the harmony is repeated over and over. This is a testament to his exemplary creativity.

In the first verse there are six-note chords used. Be careful to 'lock in' with the band on the audio. Note the use of the 4th degree (F) over the C minor chord at bar 26. This note can be found in the C minor pentatonic scale. This scale contains the notes C, E♭, F, G, B♭ and it forms much of the basis for the accompaniment figures from bar 26 onwards. This is blended with some of the chord tones of A♭ major and B♭ major.

There are quite a few slides in this section. It is important to plan which fingers will be used for each note. Some forward planning can save a great deal of time. Impractical fingerings can often limit the delivery speed of a particular passage. Also note there are many tied notes, such as in bars 30–31. This is an essential element of mature guitar playing. The double stop 4ths in bar 30 are a common rhythm approach in R 'n' B and soul music. Again, they are derived from the minor pentatonic. There are many classic Hendrix style rhythm ideas here. These can be applied to many musical situations. The rhythm part mostly uses only one or two notes at a time. Hybrid picking might be preferable for this style as the percussive sound of the pick can be more defined than flesh or nails.

The vocal and Hammond organ on this version are by the great Mike Finnigan. Mike is one of the great modern blues artists and his credits span blues and rock history.

Mike played Hammond organ on Jimi Hendrix's Electric Ladyland album. He brings a wealth of musical knowledge and invention to everything he does. Mike played with Etta James for a long time and made some classic albums with her. He's also made a notable contribution to music by Joe Cocker and currently plays with Bonnie Raitt.

The track was recorded with a real Hammond organ in Los Angeles. Mike uses a studio owned by his bandmate in The Phantom Blues Band, Johnny Lee Schell, a fabulous player in his own right.

SONG TITLE: ED SHEERAN
ALBUM: X
LABEL: LAVA / ATLANTIC
GENRE: INDIE FOLK / POP
WRITTEN BY: ED SHEERAN
GUITAR: ED SHEERAN
PRODUCER: JAKE GOSLING
UK PEAK CHART: 3

Ed Sheeran wrote 'A Team' after visiting a shelter for homeless people. He was 18 years old at the time and was very shocked by what he saw and heard. The lyrics talk about addiction to hard drugs and the upbeat nature of the song acts as a mask for the dark subject it touches upon. The song was released as a single and reached number 3 in the UK charts. 'A Team' had an AAA rating in the US, given the nature of its lyrics. Sheeran performed the song with Elton John at the 2013 Grammy ceremony.

Ed Sheeran was born in West Yorkshire in 1991 and was raised in Suffolk. He dropped out of school at 16 to pursue a career in music and moved to London. His independent releases caught the attention of Elton John and Jamie Foxx. He signed to Asylum Records in 2011. In 2012 he made a guest appearance on Taylor Swift's Red and spent much of 2013 opening her shows in the US. His second album X reached number one in the UK and US charts.

Sheeran's early influences are Van Morrison, Bob Dylan, Eric Clapton and Damien Rice.

He is one of today's most commercially successful artists.

The A Team

Ed Sheeran

Arranged by Carl Orr

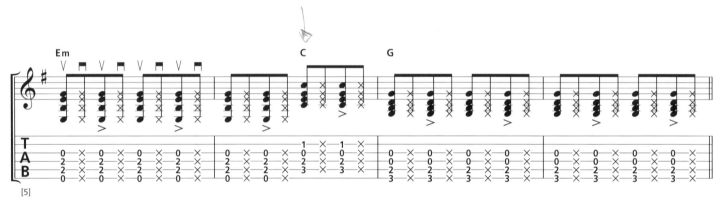

Rhythm:

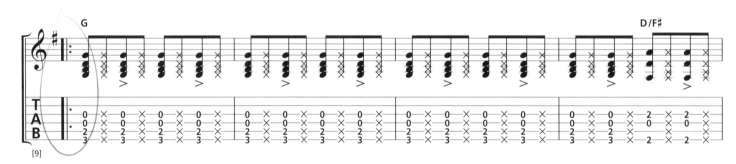

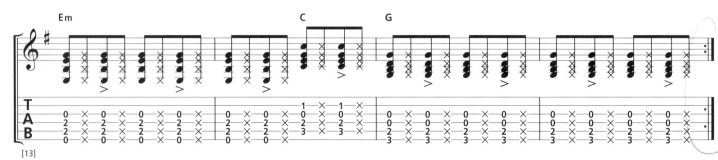

Acoustic Guitar Grade 2

12

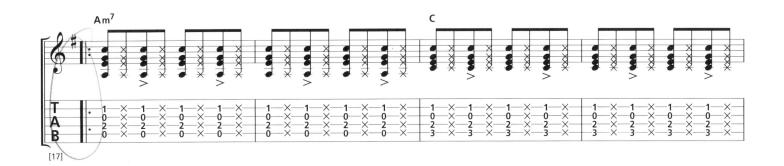

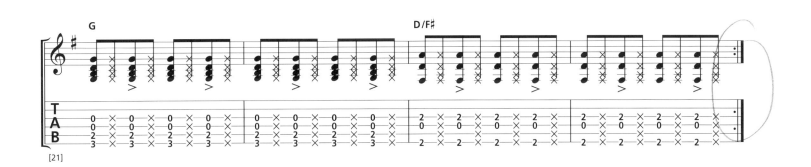

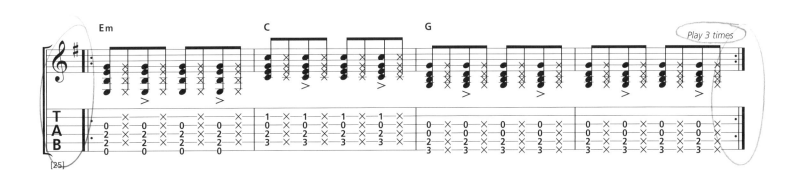

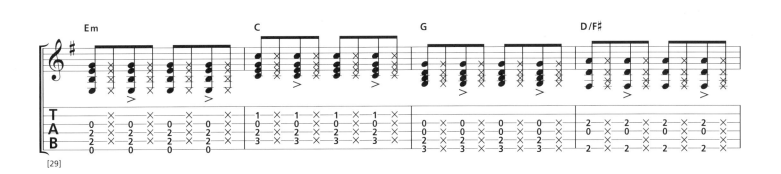

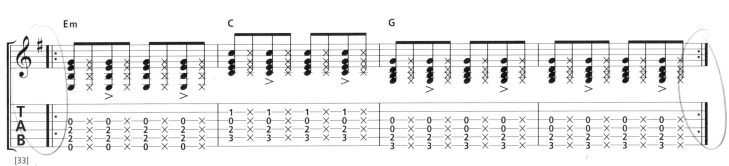

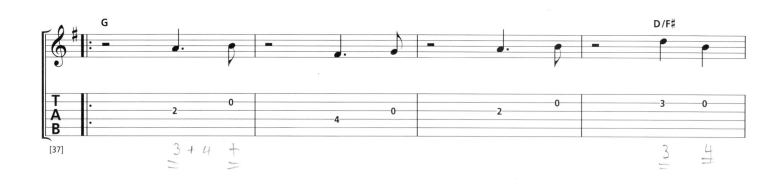

= minim rest = 2   = semibreve rest = 4

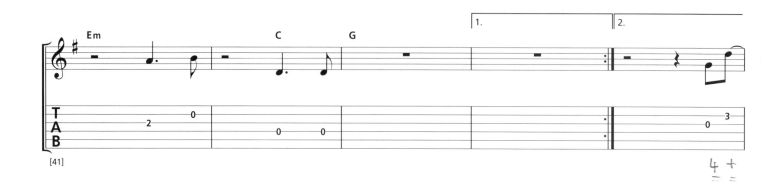

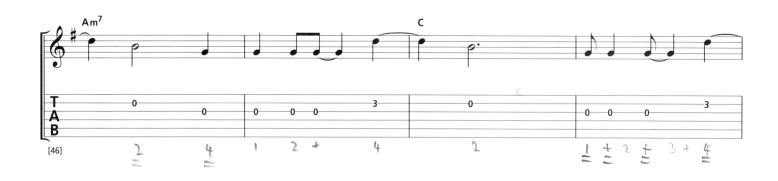

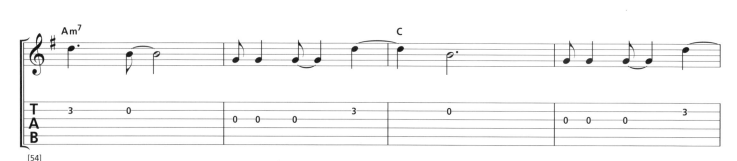

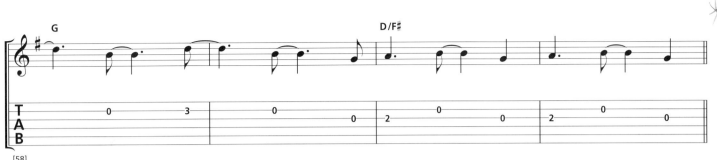

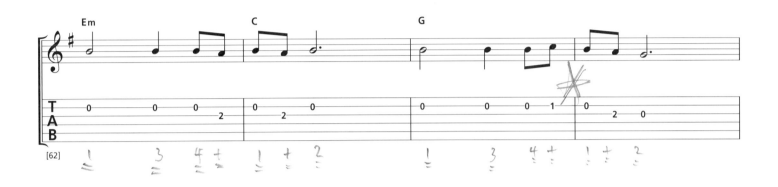

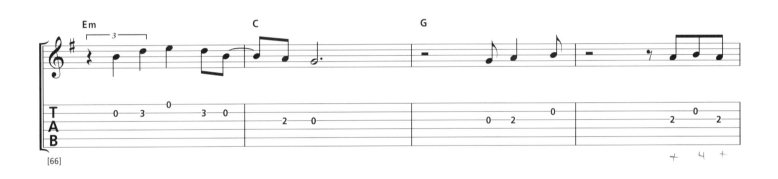

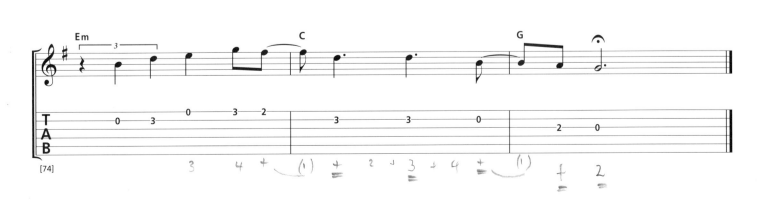

The A Team | Technical Guidance

This poignant song was originally recorded in the key of A major and played with a capo. This arrangement is in G major, so it can be played in the same way as Sheeran played it, but it will sound a tone lower.

The introduction is a brief four bars of Travis picking; the thumb plays the constant bass notes on the low E string and A string, bouncing alternately from one to the other.

The simple counterpoint of the open G and D strings is played with second (m) and first (i) fingers respectively.

Experimenting with different finger combinations will enable each student to see what works best. Apart from the intro, Ed Sheeran plays his trademark muted low-register strumming throughout, down the low end of the neck and on the lower four strings. It is executed with the thumb in a constant up/down motion, with every up stroke completely muted and serving a purely percussive function.

One of the characteristics of this approach is that the 2nd and 4th beats of each bar are accentuated, emulating the snare drum backbeat found in so much popular music. It takes sometime to get this technique feeling comfortable. However, with repetition it becomes automatic after a while.

From bar 37 the part switches to the melody. This can be played with a plectrum, with fingers or even continued with the thumb, which produces a rich, fleshy tone.

As with all of Ed Sheeran's melodies, the rhythm is the most intricate component and each phrase should be practised individually. The phrases are as follows; bars 37–42, bars 45–48, bars 49–50, bars 51–53 (first two notes) bars 53 (last note only) to 56, bars 57–61 (first two notes), bars 61 (last note only) 61–67, bars 68–71, bars 72–76.

As the song is highly syncopated, it is important to practise clapping the rhythm of each phrase separately. Once this is comfortable the pitches can be added, eventually working up to playing the whole melody. Despite its casual, effortless sound, Ed Sheeran's music requires a great deal of accuracy.

Jeff Buckley | Lover, You Should've Come Over

SONG TITLE: LOVER, YOU SHOULD'VE
COME OVER

ALBUM: GRACE

LABEL: COLUMBIA

GENRE: POP / BLUES

WRITTEN BY: JEFF BUCKLEY

GUITAR: JEFF BUCKLEY

PRODUCER: ANDY WALLACE

See note on welcome page about assessed

'Lover, You Should've Come Over' is featured on Buckley's *Grace*, his only studio album, released in 1995. The song was inspired by the end of his relationship with Rebecca Moore, his then girlfriend. The lyrics portray the feelings of unease he felt at the time and the need to outgrow certain perspectives he regarded as those of a young man.

Jeff Buckley's *Grace* is regarded as lyrical masterpiece. Buckley grew up in Orange County in California. He was the son of singer songwriter Tim Buckley and shared his father's legendary vocal ability. Before moving to New York City in 1990 he attended the Musicians' Institute in Los Angeles for a year and subsequently worked as a session guitarist. He released *Grace* in 1995. The record featured a collection of songs that showcased his considerable and singular writing style as well as his extraordinary singing ability. His work is regarded as highly influential and inspirational to many.

Jeff Buckley drowned whilst swimming in a slack water channel of the Mississippi River in May 1997. He was 29 years old and was working on his second studio album.

His premature death brought an abrupt end to a rare talent and promising career.

Lover, You Should've Come Over

Jeff Buckley

Arranged by Carl Orr

See note on welcome page about assessed and non-assessed guitar parts

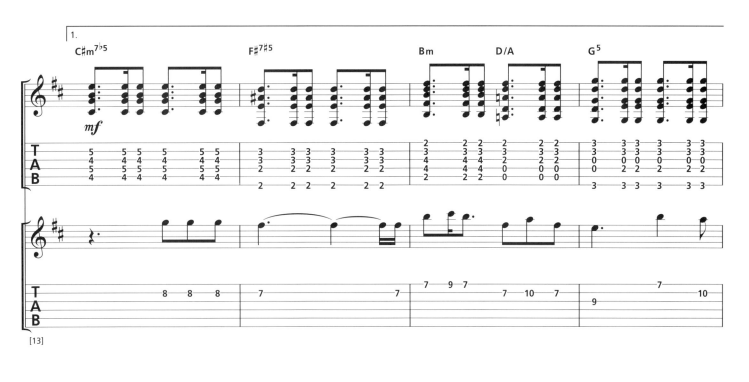

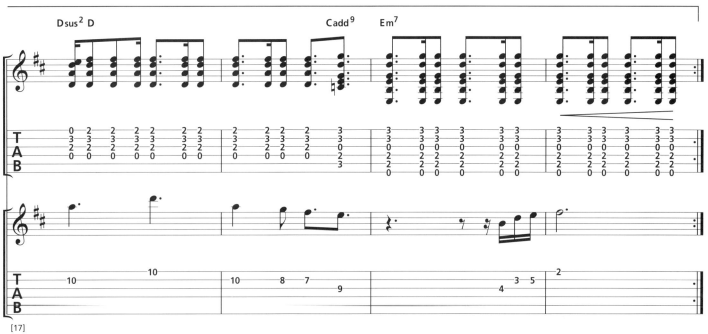

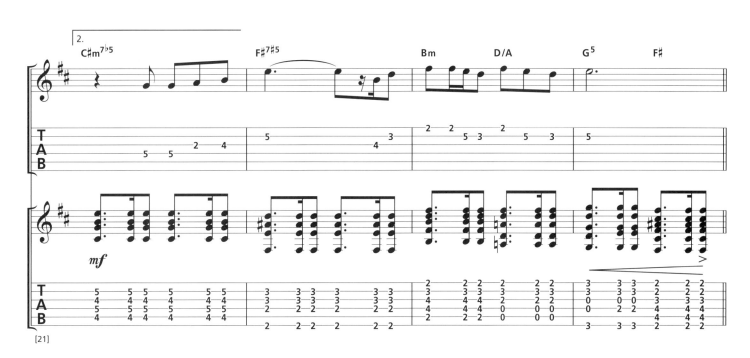

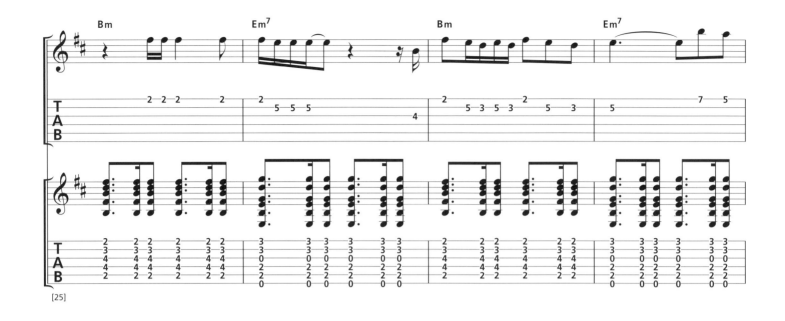

[25]

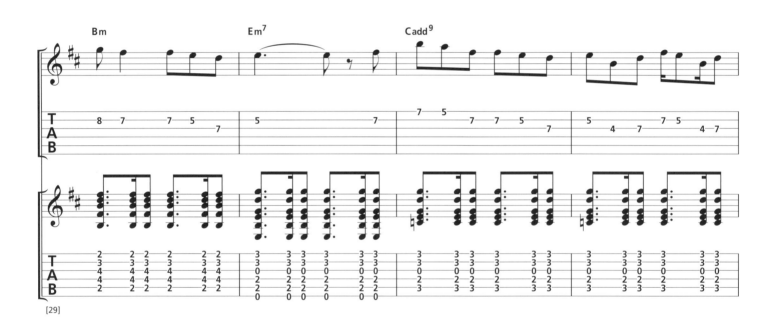

[29]

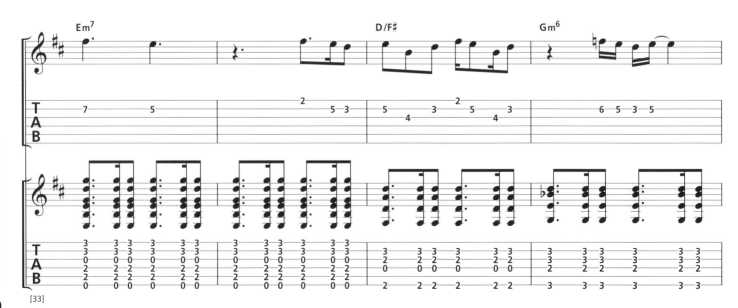

[33]

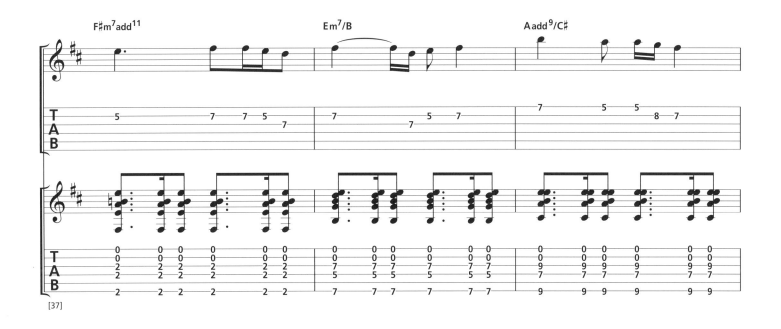

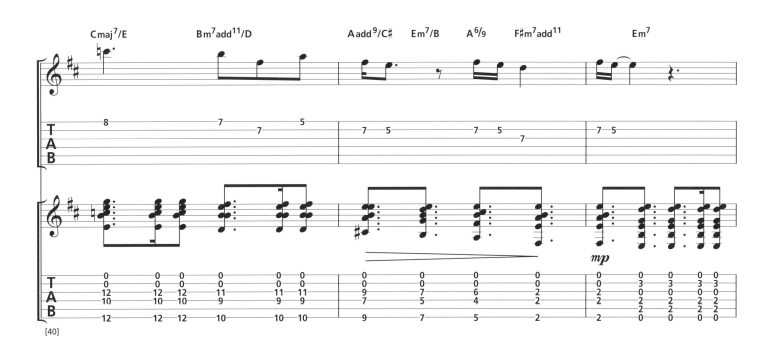

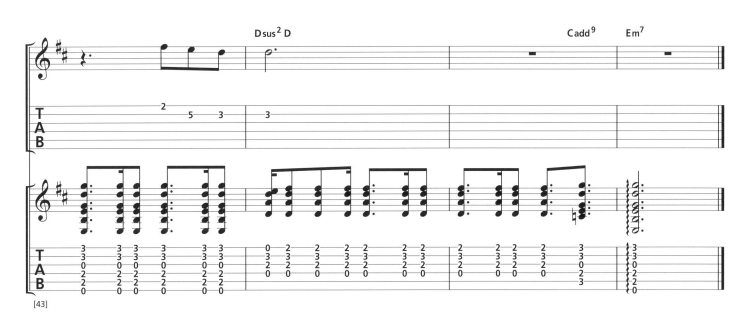

Lover, You Should've Come Over | Technical Guidance

'Lover, You Should've Come Over' features some interesting harmony. The intro and the first part of the first section share the same chords, namely two bars of D major (I/tonic) followed by two bars of Em^7 (II/supertonic) with a C major ($\flat7$/subtonic) passing chord. Then on bars 13 to 15 there is a II–V modulation to the VI chord ($C\sharp m^{7\flat5}$, $F\sharp^7$, Bm) followed by the IV chord (G major) on bar 16, with a passing Dmajor chord in between, then back to the chords of the intro again.

This angst-ridden ballad waltzes along in a gentle, relaxed 6/8, with the six beats of each bar subdivided into swung semiquavers. Listening to the track will help replicate the feel.

The picking hand should be doing a constant up/down motion in semiquavers, striking the on-the-beat notes with downstrokes and the off-the-beat notes with upstrokes. While the rhythms are simple and repetitive, $Cadd^9$ chord on the upbeat of five in bars 2, 6, 10 and 18 can be tricky to place.

From the second time bar at bar 21, the part switches to the melody. While technically simple, it is rhythmically advanced, so it is advisable to clap the rhythm of each tricky-looking bar in turn before playing it; such as bars 22, 23, 25, 26, 27, 32, 34, 35, 37, 38, 39.

The song features many interesting chords, so it can be rewarding and fascinating to look at the teacher's part from bar 25 onwards. While this part, you may find a few useful and unique chords that can be used in the future, plus, it is always satisfying and confidence-boosting to know all the chords to any song you learn.

Otis Redding | (Sittin' On) The Dock Of The Bay

SONG TITLE: (SITTIN' ON)
THE DOCK OF THE BAY
ALBUM: THE DOCK OF THE BAY
LABEL: STAX / VOLT
GENRE: RHYTHM AND BLUES /
SOUL
WRITTEN BY: OTIS REDDING AND
STEVE CROPPER
GUITAR: STEVE CROPPER
PRODUCER: OTIS REDDING AND
STEVE CROPPER

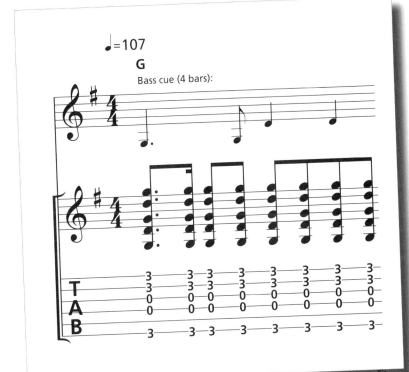

Otis Redding wrote the lyrics to 'Sittin' on the Dock of the Bay' whilst staying at a rented houseboat in Sausalito, California, in August 1967. He completed the song in December of 1967 in collaboration with Steve Crooper who was a producer for Stax records and guitarist for Booker T and the M.G's. Redding died in a plane crash days later. Cropper mixed the song and included the sound of seagulls and waves requested by Redding before his death. These were the sounds he recalled from staying in the houseboat.

The melancholy of the lyrics, the emotive vocal delivery and the succinct guitar playing transformed the song into an instant classic. It is one of the most performed songs of the 20th century.

Redding is regarded as a seminal voice in American popular music. He was born in Dawson, Georgia, in 1941 and died aged 26, in Monona, Wisconsin, on December 10th 1967. He also recorded classics such as 'Respect' and 'Try A Little Tenderness'. Soul and the Stax Sound have been significantly influenced by his powerful singing and writing styles.

'Sittin' On The Dock Of The Bay' has been covered by a multitude of artists including Sammy Haggar, Michael Bolton and Justin Timberlake.

(Sittin' On) The Dock Of The Bay

Otis Redding

Arranged by Andy G Jones

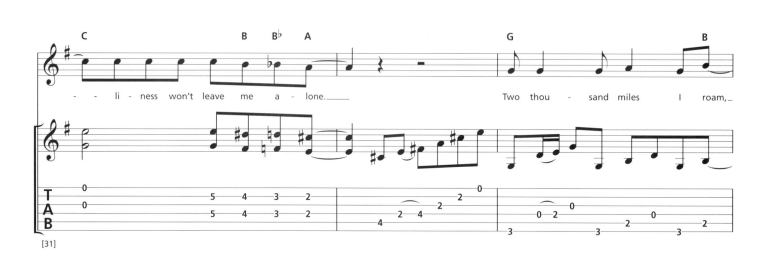

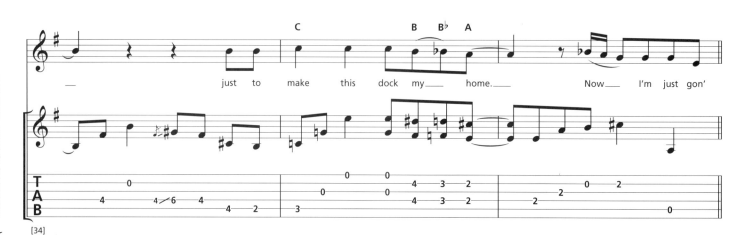

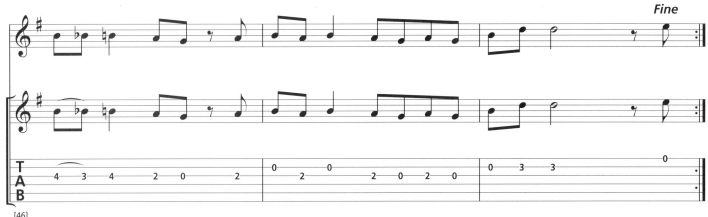

(Sittin' On) The Dock Of The Bay | Technical Guidance

'(Sittin' On) The Dock Of The Bay' was written by Otis Redding and rhythm guitar great Steve Cropper.

The chord changes are surprisingly bold – the change from G major to E major is an example.

E is the 6th degree of G. You would expect a minor chord on this root, not the major we find here. It's more unusual because it doesn't resolve down to an A minor chord, acting as a secondary dominant. The fact that the tune oscillates between the G major and E major chords is a striking detail.

The rhythm guitar playing on this song forms the cornerstone of many professional guitarist's approach to accompaniment. Note how clearly Cropper outlines the chords whilst retaining a bluesy, rootsy soul guitar feel. Often only one or two notes are being played somehow sounding more defined than if chords with four or more notes where used. These can sound muddy in this kind of context and take vital space for the other instruments. A large part of the art of playing with other people is learning when to leave space for their input.

Many of the fills from Cropper's original recording are included in this version. Note the use of the 4th to the 3rd degree on the A major chord. The rhythm pattern at bar 13 has become an iconic lick. Note how it lands on the 9th degree of the E major chord. These are masterful and subtle touches.

Cropper's use of double stop 6ths to follow the chromatically descending chords from C major to A major (bar 35) is also another cornerstone of soul guitar.

The whistling melody is incorporated in the outro (Coda/bar 45).

Whilst the tune can be played with any of the right hand techniques discussed so far, a plectrum is recommended because it gives clear articulation.

SONG TITLE: WONDERWALL
ALBUM: (WHAT'S THE STORY)
MORNING GLORY? / 1995
LABEL: CREATION
GENRE: BRITPOP
WRITTEN BY: NOEL GALLAGHER
GUITAR: NOEL GALLAGHER
PRODUCER: OWEN MORRIS AND
NOEL GALLAGHER
UK PEAK CHART: 2

'Wonderwall' is the third single taken from Oasis' *(What's The Story) Morning Glory?*. It was a huge hit worldwide and it remains the band's most popular song.

It was written by Noel Gallagher and the lyrics describe the arrival of an imaginary friend who comes to save the writer from himself. The song was covered numerous times since its release in 1995.

Oasis were formed in Manchester in 1991. The band had a meteoric rise to fame and the Gallagher brothers, Liam and Noel, were frequently featured in tabloid newspapers due to their sibling disputes and wild behaviour.

The band's sound borrowed heavily from The Beatles' tradition but it did so with added qualities and attitude. They experienced many personnel changes, eventually leading to Noel Gallagher's departure in 2009 after a row with brother Liam.

The band was in constant rivalry with peers Blur in the heady days of Britpop. Their 1997 album *Be Here Now* was the fastest selling album in the UK's chart history. A record they held until Adele's release of *25* in November 2015.

Wonderwall

Oasis

Arranged by James Betteridge

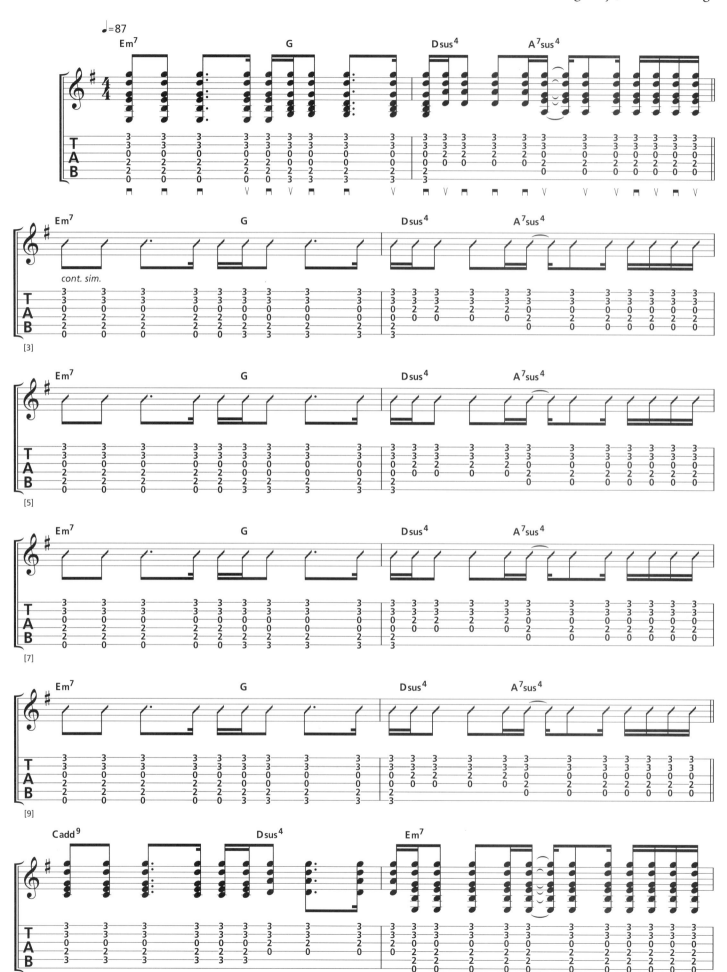

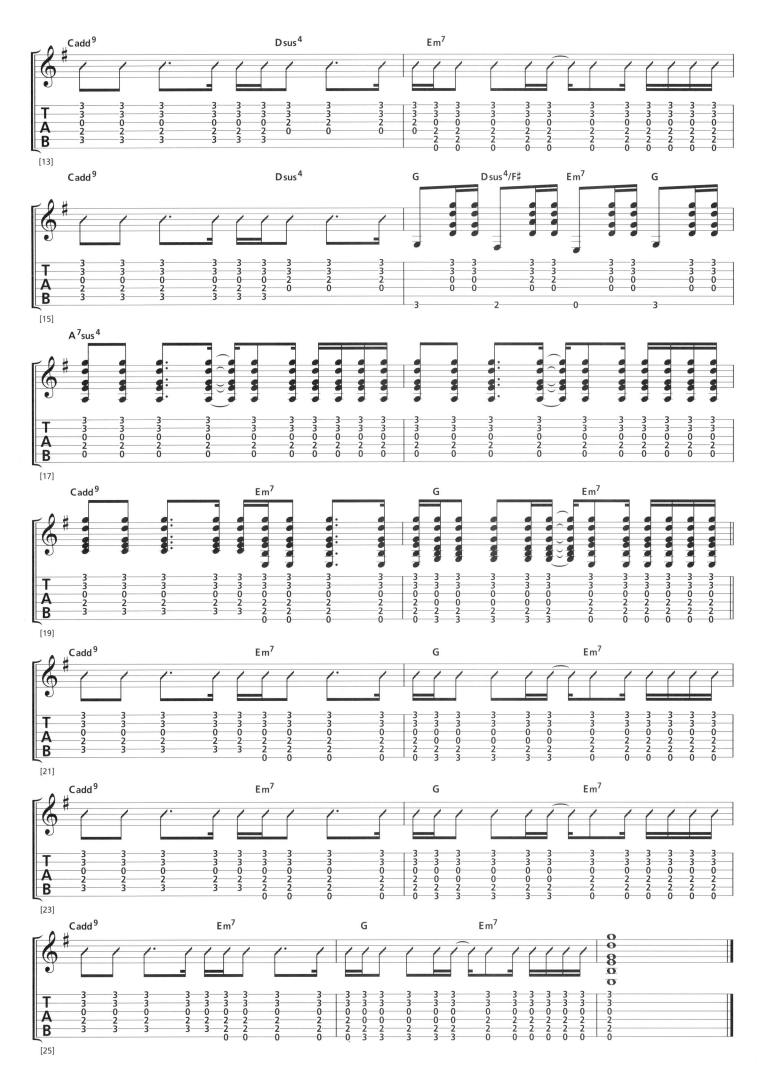

Wonderwall | Technical Guidance

Wonderwall is originally recorded in F♯ minor and would require a capo at the second fret to play the part's specific chord shapes. This arrangement has been transposed down a tone to the key of E minor to avoid having to use a capo.

The chords in the song are Em^7(I/tonic), G major (♭III/mediant), $Dsus^4$ (♭VII/subtonic), A^7sus^4 (IV/subdominant) and $Cadd^9$ (♭VI/submediant). If we think of each chord as a triad (three note chords) we can see where they belong within the E minor scale. Below is a diagram to help illustrate this.

The E natural minor scale:

I	II	♭III	IV	V	♭VI	♭VII
E min	F♯ dim	G maj	A min	B min	C maj	D maj
E min		G maj	A min		C maj	D maj

This abridged arrangement focuses on the intro, verse and chorus of the song. In sections where the guitar part is repetitive the notation has been changed to rhythm slashes. This will make it clearer to identify where it changes, making it easier to follow.

The song features a 16th-note strumming pattern played on an acoustic guitar, which has become a classic amongst aspiring guitarists. Take note of the suggested strumming pattern above the tab. It is advisable to use the underlying 16th note rhythm as a guide for the strumming hand, starting slowly.

To help create a smooth transition between the chord changes, it is advisable to keep the 3rd and 4th finger of the fretting hand planted on the B and E string, as these notes (D and G) are common to the chord shapes utilised. There are many live versions available on line that will help as guides.

To get an even-sounding attack across the strings, try to experiment with different gauge picks. There is no right or wrong, but a thinner plectrum, which has a little give in it, will generally help achieve this.

SONG TITLE: WILD WOOD

ALBUM: WILD WOOD / 1993

LABEL: GO! DISCS

GENRE: ROCK

WRITTEN BY: PAUL WELLER

GUITAR: PAUL WELLER

PRODUCER: PAUL WELLER AND

BRENDAN LYNCH

UK PEAK CHART: 14

Paul Weller's 'Wild Wood' is featured on the album of the same name, released in 1993. It is Weller's second solo release. The song is a typical Weller ballad, featuring a soulful vocal and haunting instrumentation.

Paul Weller's writing is deeply rooted in British culture and he is often mentioned as a significant influence to the Britpop generation. He was born near Woking in 1958.

His early influences were The Beatles and The Who. He formed The Jam in the early 70's and the band became a significant exponent of the New Wave sound of the late 70's. The band's popularity increased and with it Weller's eagerness to explore different sounds, leading to his decision to disband The Jam and form the soul outfit The Style Council in 1983. This came as a shock to band members and fans alike. By the early 80's The Jam were an English household name.

Paul Weller started a successful solo career in 1990 and has released 12 albums to date. He is considered a significant figure in English songwriting.

Wild Wood

Paul Weller

Arranged by James Betteridge

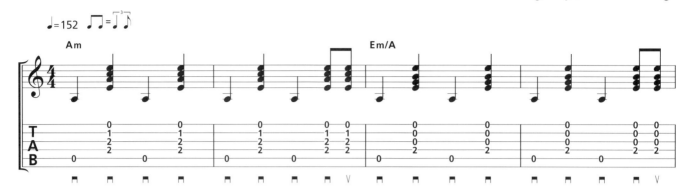

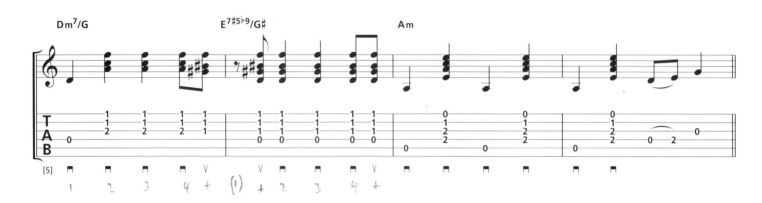

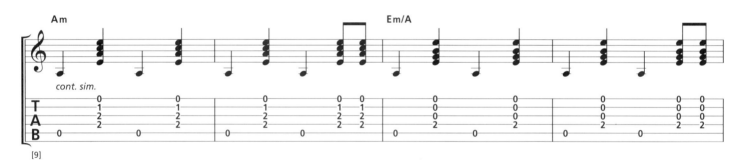

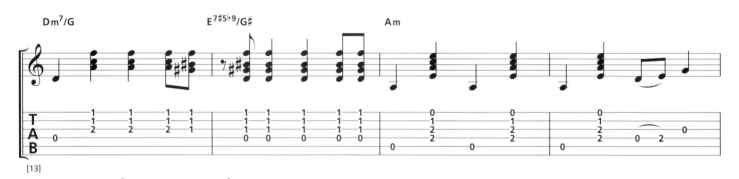

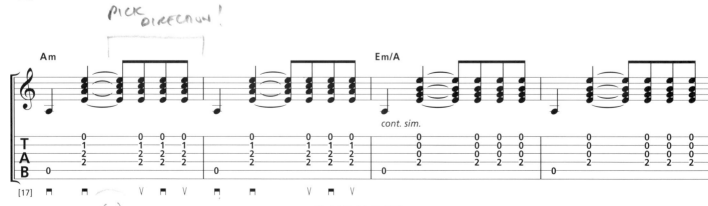

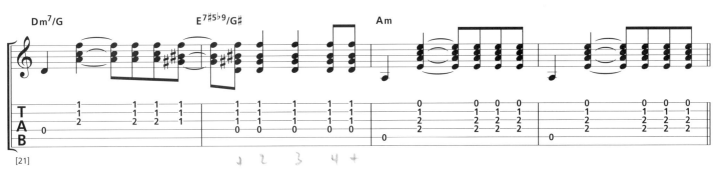

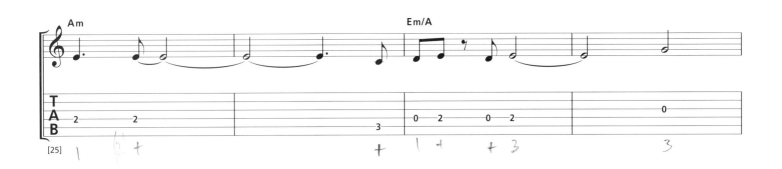

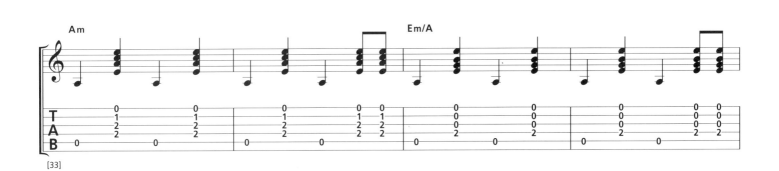

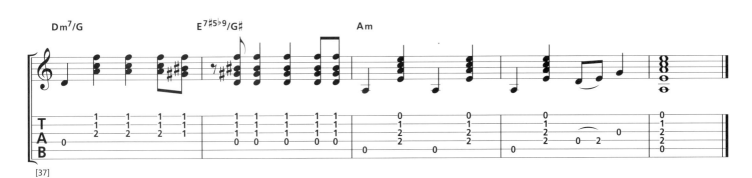

Wild Wood | Technical Guidance

Wild Wood's original recording is in the key of B minor. This arrangement is in the key of A minor to avoid having to use a capo. To play along with the original recording, simply place a capo on the second fret.

The song is based around four chords, A minor (I/tonic) , Em/A (Em with an A as the lowest note) Dm^7 (IV/subdominant) and $E^{7\flat9\sharp5}$/G$\sharp$ (V/dominant). The latter looks like a very daunting chord voicing but without the alterations ($\sharp$5 and $\flat$9) we are left with an E^7/G$\sharp$ (1st inversion) chord. The non-diatonic E^7, instead of the diatonic E minor creates a stronger resolution from the V chord to the I chord. The chord voicing in the transcription is a rootless voicing as there is no E.

The A natural minor scale:

I	II	$\flat$III	IV	V	$\flat$VI	$\flat$VII
A min	B dim	C maj	D min	E min	F maj	G maj
A min			D min	E min		

The tempo of the piece is quite quick at 152 bpm and is swung (implying the first quaver feels longer than the second one). It is advisable to listen to the track featuring this feel in order to get familiar with its effect.

The rhythm is mainly based around a four bar repeated pattern containing crotchets and swung quavers. The suggested strumming pattern is written above the tablature. It is advisable to use the underlying swung quaver rhythm as a guide for the strumming hand.

The rhythm varies from bar 17. Take note of the suggested strumming pattern written above the tablature.

From bars 25 to 33, there is an eight bar solo. The solo follows the vocal melody line with a couple of embellishments. It is important to let notes ring for their full length and to avoid unwanted strings.

Technical Exercises

In this section, you will be asked to play a selection of exercises, chosen by the examiner, from each of the groups below.

All exercises need to be played in straight feel, in the keys, octaves and tempos shown.

You can use your book in the exam for Groups A and B. Group C must be performed from memory.

Note that Groups A and B need to be played to a click and any fingerings shown are suggestions only.

Group A: Scales

The tempo for this group is ♩=66 bpm.

1. D major scale ✗ *See Other notes*

2. B♭ major scale ✗ *See Other notes.*

3. B natural minor scale

4. G natural minor scale

5. B harmonic minor scale

Technical Exercises

6. G harmonic minor scale

7. C mixolydian mode

8. C melodic minor scale

9. Chromatic scale on D

10. Chromatic scale on B♭

Group B: Arpeggios

The tempo for this group is ♩=63 bpm.

1. D major arpeggio

2. D major arpeggio

3. B♭ major arpeggio

4. B♭ major arpeggio

5. B minor arpeggio

6. B minor arpeggio

7. G minor arpeggio

8. G minor arpeggio

9. C dominant 7 (C7) arpeggio

Group C: Chord Voicings

In the exam you will be asked to play, from memory, your choice of one chord voicing from each of the following exercises, without the aid of a backing track or metronome. However, for practice purposes a demonstration of the chords played to a metronome click is available in the downloadable audio.

1. C dominant 7 (C7)

2. C minor 6 (Cm6)

Sight Reading

In this section you have a choice between either a sight reading test or an improvisation and interpretation test (see facing page).

The examiner will ask you which one you wish to choose before commencing. Once you have decided you cannot change your mind.

In the sight reading test, the examiner will give you a 4–6 bar melody in the key of B♭ major or D major. You will first be given 90 seconds to practise, after which the examiner will play the backing track twice. The first time is for you to practise and the second time is for you to perform the final version for the exam. For each playthrough, the backing track will begin with a one bar count-in. The tempo is ♩=60–95.

During the practice time, you will be given the choice of a metronome click throughout or a one bar count-in at the beginning.

The backing track is continuous, so once the first playthrough has finished, the count-in of the second playing will start immediately.

Sight Reading | Example 1

Please note: The test shown is an example. The examiner will give you a different version in the exam.

Sight Reading | Example 2

Please note: The test shown is an example. The examiner will give you a different version in the exam.

Improvisation & Interpretation

In the improvisation and interpretation test, the examiner will give you a 4–6 bar chord progression in the key of B♭ major or D major. You will first be given 90 seconds to practise, after which the examiner will play the backing track twice. The first time is for you to practise and the second time is for you to perform the final version for the exam. For each playthrough, the backing track will begin with a one bar count-in. The tempo is ♩=60–95.

During the practice time, you will be given the choice of a metronome click throughout or a one bar count-in at the beginning.

The backing track is continuous, so once the first playthrough has finished, the count-in of the second playing will start immediately.

You are only required to improvise single note melodies.

Improvisation & Interpretation | Example 1

Please note: The test shown is an example. The examiner will give you a different version in the exam.

Improvisation & Interpretation | Example 2

Please note: The test shown is an example. The examiner will give you a different version in the exam.

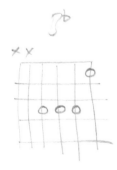

Ear Tests

In this section, there are two ear tests:

- Melodic Recall
- Chord Recognition

You will find one example of each type of test printed below and you will need to perform both of them in the exam.

Test 1: Melodic Recall

The examiner will play you a 2 bar diatonic melody in the key of C major with a range up to a fourth. The first note will be the root note. You will hear the test twice, each time with a one bar count-in, then you will hear a further one bar count-in after which you will need to play the melody to the click. The tempo is ♩ = 95 bpm.

It is acceptable to play over the track as it is being played as well as practising after the second playthough. The length of time available after the second playthrough is pre-recorded on the audio track so the count-in may begin while you are still practising.

Please note: The test shown is an example. The examiner will give you a different version in the exam.

Test 2: Chord Recognition

The examiner will play you a sequence of chords, each with a C root note. You will hear the chord sequence twice, each time with a one bar count-in. You will then be asked to identify the chord quality of each chord, from a choice of major, minor, diminished, augmented and dominant 7th. The tempo is ♩ = 95 bpm.

Please note: The test shown is an example. The examiner will give you a different version in the exam.

General Musicianship Questions

The final part of your exam is the General Musicianship Questions section, which features 5 questions relating to one of your choice of the performance pieces.

1. You will be asked a question relating to the harmony from a section of one of your pieces.

2. You will be asked a question relating to the melody in a section of one of your pieces.

3. You will be asked a question relating to the rhythms used in a section of one of your pieces.

4. You will be asked a question relating to the technical requirements of one of your pieces.

5. You will be asked a question relating to the genre of one of your pieces.

Entering Rockschool Exams

Entering a Rockschool exam is easy, just go online and follow our simple six step process. All details for entering online, dates, fees, regulations and Free Choice pieces can be found at *www.rslawards.com*

- All candidates should ensure they bring their own Grade syllabus book to the exam or have their KR app ready and the full book downloaded.

- All Grade 6–8 candidates must ensure that they bring valid photo ID to their exam.

- Candidates will receive their exam results (and certificates if applicable) a maximum of 3 weeks after their exam. If nothing has been received after this time then please call +44 (0)345 460 4747 or email to *info@rslawards.com*

Marking Schemes

GRADE EXAMS | DEBUT TO GRADE 5 *

ELEMENT	PASS	MERIT	DISTINCTION
Performance Piece 1	12–14 out of 20	15–17 out of 20	18+ out of 20
Performance Piece 2	12–14 out of 20	15–17 out of 20	18+ out of 20
Performance Piece 3	12–14 out of 20	15–17 out of 20	18+ out of 20
Technical Exercises	9–10 out of 15	11–12 out of 15	13+ out of 15
Sight Reading _or_ Improvisation & Interpretation	6 out of 10	7–8 out of 10	9+ out of 10
Ear Tests	6 out of 10	7–8 out of 10	9+ out of 10
General Musicianship Questions	3 out of 5	4 out of 5	5 out of 5
TOTAL MARKS	60%+	74%+	90%+

GRADE EXAMS | GRADES 6–8

ELEMENT	PASS	MERIT	DISTINCTION
Performance Piece 1	12–14 out of 20	15–17 out of 20	18+ out of 20
Performance Piece 2	12–14 out of 20	15–17 out of 20	18+ out of 20
Performance Piece 3	12–14 out of 20	15–17 out of 20	18+ out of 20
Technical Exercises	9–10 out of 15	11–12 out of 15	13+ out of 15
Quick Study Piece	6 out of 10	7–8 out of 10	9+ out of 10
Ear Tests	6 out of 10	7–8 out of 10	9+ out of 10
General Musicianship Questions	3 out of 5	4 out of 5	5 out of 5
TOTAL MARKS	60%+	74%+	90%+

PERFORMANCE CERTIFICATES | DEBUT TO GRADE 8 *

ELEMENT	PASS	MERIT	DISTINCTION
Performance Piece 1	12–14 out of 20	15–17 out of 20	18+ out of 20
Performance Piece 2	12–14 out of 20	15–17 out of 20	18+ out of 20
Performance Piece 3	12–14 out of 20	15–17 out of 20	18+ out of 20
Performance Piece 4	12–14 out of 20	15–17 out of 20	18+ out of 20
Performance Piece 5	12–14 out of 20	15–17 out of 20	18+ out of 20
TOTAL MARKS	60%+	75%+	90%+

* Note that there are no Debut Vocal exams.

Copyright Information